Lucidities

Lucidities

Toni Hurford

ISBN: 979-8-3884-6927-4

God lives in every kind person.

Leo Tolstoy, Wise Thoughts for Every Day, 3 January

CONTENTS

A Sea

Perhaps
       a sea of light
                surges   swells
storms sands
       seethes   in   retreat
singing
      lightly chained
            wild home to herself

She crashes shores material
               solid grounds shape song
North   German
         Our Sea   Southern
Pacific even Tranquility
          or sand
sea remains sea

Though sometimes I have found may forget   b e l i e v e
land's wooing   craven wish for moisture cloud distilled to
ease rigidity   balm he'd hold landlocked   irons bound
form given

Eyes of clay
words of stone
trap with firm tongue
juggle with soiled hands,
to deal dwelling in dells
gutters
the hollows of earth
sieved by marl flesh
forgetting current
swell

Now a river
lake
a puddle

cut off

    trickle of sea self
              sometimes
                    torrent
                          bleeding
                                coastward
                                      when she can

    Remember
              tear-
                    drop
    the home
            you're part of

Tynemouth, Any Mouth

The gull cat-mewls a cry-baby protest
as it tugs at the grass, stuck in its fact,
fractal, part of the wave, particle surfing
its place in the blast, the explosion of fact.
The element stew of each filament hair
charged to glow in the current of time's
time lapsed fire-fall tail swallow act.
We explore how it burns, what we may be.
Amber warning, let's get back to the facts,
the star scattered sea, dancing with light,
eternal, the heart of all in each flash.
This is my cry, my tug at this earth,
the best I can do at this now on the wave,
part of the sparkle of a sea in a sun.

lost love song

i hadn't really reached you yet
i wasn't up to you
even though i'd passed myself
to burn a summit sun
distant from myself you see
distant from the world
i didn't have the faith you know
to share with you my poem
to say the gentle words of love
to still the thunder of our blood
to let us be our own

discourse

the shallow excuses of literalists
intricate and pretty
a frosted window
a garden at dawn in stasis
dangerous
to buds and immaturity
hanging with spiders' webs
by a thread
because in the night we said so

icy echo of a moment
out of context
of the breath's agenda
penetrating from the surface
a cold carapace
real temporary winter
death haunts the skin
lingering when gone
as we jog along in fullness
to the reprise of the sun

a classic mistake

love boundaried
discovers blind edges
as hate

Supernova

Was it for this, all past shining,
that his light censored heart went critical,
burst social containment,
true message fractured dark.

The urgent nonsense of himself, collapse,
to black hole singularity. Hell perhaps.

Awareness balanced at event horizon,
held on cosmic scales,
an unexpected black mass,
cold regret - what could be next?

As echoes play on his corona,
glimpses of love, ache.
He sorts this information into order
to understand his own distress.

Bracing for the long fought darkness,
his only path is to accept.

They Think

They think they know you know
They think they do
They've got what they've heard
Such reliable word
That they think they know
All about you

So they'll act and imply
Without fear of reply
As no one ever bothered
To put it to you

They are quite certain
They know who you are
Though the *who* gets lost
You're now more of a *what*
As they comment around and about
Thoughtless of you

They seem to rely
On a fear to reply
That you're dumb to their jibes
That real life passes you by

They think you're wrong about you
That you're not true
That you'd be you
If you were their you
If only you knew how to be you

But they don't know

You do

LILLY
4112*

My every day is typical of you.
That is what you do.
Your enchanted headband
mutes whispers of the gods.

Before, I worshipped living to sleeplessness,
unable to let go. Hypnos left me,
a play thing for his kin.
Pan nodded by.

So, seven years I spent in shelter,
'Nil periculum' your motto.
'Heal thyself' my own.

I did too; Magic band removed.
Grasses blew, sparkle in the waves.
Everything intense, everything alive.
Worship renewed.

Then, Bacon peeled my eyes.
A great storm blew.
I knew one greater than you.

Now, I eat your body daily.
Communion, of sorts,
of human gathering.
Antidote to fear: theirs, my own.

A Golden Calf,
a scientific-fetish god,
you colour me.

My worship is not all mine.

My god.

Winter

As the months approach year end,
days bleak, dark takes hold.

Stark images of leafless trees,
black against the autumn sky,
bend cheer away.

My life feels fallen into winter,
not due to natural rhythm
but medicine.

Silent watcher in life's cinema,
wrapped in freezing fog,
feelings permafrozen.

Each day, just out of reach,
listening for the sun
breaking in the words.

Neuroleptic

waking I have not woken
sleeping is not sleep
the shutters   they   are   broken
with this pill   I cannot weep

they say that I am broken
held together with a sweet
to keep me low   even   frozen
a dawn no one ever greets

Incarnation

Born, this is the meat of it,
the meta too for some.

This feast of flesh.

Which way does it go, control,
flesh to spirit, or spirit flesh.

A balance must be struck, you say.

Yet the dreams of the body are relentless,
so much time spent over this temple's ownership.

A war, it can be, no less.
God, gods, demons or just some conflict that makes sense.

Written into flesh and flesh to self.

I've cycled through human forms, ideas
of myself, poses struck,

a life's Dante-esque mug shots for God,
GPS stamped holistically for judgement,

and my own

and the last laugh,
that of others,

who'll join the feast upon yourself
with their set menu,

as if they knew.

dream

all the magpies were in pairs
nestled together in the cold
but when i looked i felt
nothing could be done for sorrow
and besides, looking back,
they weren't magpies but puffins.

A Different Slant

The colliery road sweeps a minor curve
over a bridge, beneath an embankment,
from the top of which, far above the deep dead pit,
a pony looks down his nose, majestic.
I'm driving, not fast, and for a flash,
as I look in his eyes, see he's been waiting,
just for me to pass.

Another day at road end sands,
sea calm, tide out
light perfect but camera-less,
the world sings me to a halt.
To share a minute's seal pup stare.
She shallows ducking, me counting whiskers.
Transfixed. Then walking on.
Wondering later
if there's etiquette
for such exchanges.

One summer's day,
reading wisdom on grass in the sun,
a spider walks on the page.
I imagine its view,
and for a moment lose
who is who.

Bourne
(after the films)

some unholy myth of achievement
rat champion of every maze
we wish you well in your bereavement
reborn we know our loss of face

yet sacred is your perseverance
you've learned what rats may not outrun
our paradoxical convergence
but what of those you do 'anon'?

true bearing may hide in refusal
to play the game the way you're placed
identity's smile found fraternal
life's risk borne, a whole new face

Of Course

A butterfly eye in my own hurricane,
sails becalmed behind a storm face.
All at sea, Tyne tide caught,
to fortune seek the Sea King's wind source.

Storm system storm fought, wind thrown,
tacked back from a flat earth edge-fall,
deciding to face flutter-by strangeness,
took bad harbour with a taxonomist stranger.

Whose ordered chaos doubled my strength,
summoned my false heart to its own edge,
scream-vision driven against her Black Middens,
eye open to eye's substance in the wind's path.

So, the rational alchemy of medicine men
was stirred to guide this cyclone ride blow out.
found storm flung, beach scattered, ocean wide.
Where regathering wind sense amidst the gale

I must stitch sail of booty and remaining rags,
to catch best blows under strange scarred skies.
Hope's heading to chart trade lanes
between my mother country and these colonies of me.

Rimbaud, Zen

Absolutely modern,
always present,
breathe in, breathe out,
now . . . and now . . . and now . . .

The Natural Word

Frosted orange eye shadow
with copper underwing,
tonight perhaps.
Fritillaries of maiden hair,
the very latest thing.
Golden brown hairstreak
with ringlets shower down.
Large blue eyes lined smoky.
Lips luscious, peach blossom blush.
Buff arches in high heels.
Everything so right,
she uses the world's vocabulary
to bend its grammar rules.
Go downy with her,
wary of thorns.

Leda

(after 'Leda and the Swan' by John Bellany)

Mirror mute, used, hair a mess
your long life-loving meander
has reached its destination,
chameleon clay fired and set.
A pale-faced pen-mask make-up,
no need for Bjorkian feather dress,
your glide speaks of your loyalties
to ideals made real meta-human.
Yet glance-eyed I know a limber self
for all it shores up all your doors
to seal a sacrifice to changeling gods.
Irregular love is all some will see,
amidst a crazy paved bohemia
you'll have to co-create, shameless,
paddling furiously underneath, to fight
how every other encounter will set
your Greek irregularity of mind,
paranoia turned paraphilia,
into a gilded modern sense.

maid

your satin dress across yourself
swishy in your stars
all victories have come to this
a winner gives their sword
eyes upon infinity
somewhere in the clouds
lost in others' certainties
tethered to this ground
french fancy playfulness
false paradise of petty nicenesses
dream child of another moon
you forgot the rule of rule
or this a meaty lesson
wolves can't help consume

travesty

this backward subject
speaks a strange language, poetry
free now, to be
now he has been discounted
mayhap the court fool
not quite a looking glass, Sir, Madam
everything reversed
reverie of the deep, beneath beneath
mermaid vision
glass bottomed glimmer in the weeds
a dream
out of reach, the air around her wobbles
as she breathes

throw her in the dungeon
make her work the kitchens
you must protect your throne

A Sonnet

Speak strange of Supermoons and she-men
spun from silly misheard sisters' stories.
Staff dressed by distaff side to serve, soul
submitted, sold, simply to be sincere,
near to themselves, my most precious me dis-
played, auto turned inside out, you see,
no turning back, a one way trip down this
Moebius Strip, twisted into what my
satisfied chiral bi-polarity
didn't want, need, but took the time to read
in the mirror of my dream of being.
Strange songs are sacred in their minor key
of man, don't fear, my sweet, weavers who say
your right, in their mirror, smells sinister.

Transreality

Weird sister? No, your best sense is released.
Soul whisper, condensed and born mid-life.
Rules demanded your breathing be self-ceased.
Set free now, you were never your own wife.

Hey, why not be yourself as another's,
natural, with some woman's golden hair.
No search for strength required, remember
your flame freed spirit's ease is fair.

For whilst they'll never know your strength to find
yourself beneath, it's not so strange to be
in search of shape down this our knotted wind.
It's quite normal as any me should see.

We struggle down a shady path toward
a dream of form, sure to be imperfect.

A Reunion

"For whosoever would save his soul shall lose it" Mark 8:35

It was with shock I found that student passport pic.
I took several strips, to find a face I could accept.
All youth's spirit given a safe porcelain glaze,
dull-doll, numb to lack in the numb-mask he portrayed.
Compare my latter decade's snaps, the very
picture of a person, happy, warm, connected,
dolling it up heart-free beyond my taught horizon
- as a young woman - I only start to see me now,
reconcile how a youth's treasure was spent to hide,
dial myself into combinations, self safe-shut,
to step out unfussed, mirror of what was wonted,
model of a grammar of needs need inverted.
How this heart's been tempered, in absence grew,
my dress has uncovered me, is this me, with you.

Plight

Is it vulgar, to gambol, on both sides
of a sacred marriage? Not one thing or the other.
There is a breath of spring and a knell of winter,
the buzz of a party and a wedding altercation.
I'm unsure I'm invited to either.
Small inside my puff pastry story
I'm blowing on some ember - sometimes a flame,
sometimes cinders - dizzy oscillator.
Truth in both - true in neither.
A neuter case to curse the wedding night.
Unless, dance card spirited away, secreted
in some fold, I turn toward my song,
party of one, alone, seeking paradise.
A veil lifted, falls to outward celebration.

Girlhood XXIV

second bloom in a mirror
she steps forward in pigtails
embraces temporal dissonance
this previously quite taboo
life bound in a double plait

summer time

as time slips i sip the hours
suntime nonsense flower
dreamer amidst woody bowers
weekend woman springing out
feeling her breathy path by breeze
toward a sun stance
hip swung nonchalance
among happiness in bluebells

———

i, not quite, of the bluebells
increasingly away with the flowers
giddy, sing-song, gone wrong
gossamer rhyme blossom
coming alive

not so much singer as song
not so much goer as gone

waiter upon bees
turning to be

cowslip, daff
meadow sweet
buttercup

flowering at last
a rose

as if

Paper

It is not first words.
Nor any we have spoken.
But that we may, hoping . . .

* * *

I am lost in this world,
in all the worlds within
in all the words spoken
the storm they ride,
their wind.

But at any moment
may forget the whirl,
remember silent arbour,
rooted anchorage,
quite still.

Whether in clearing
on wood path
or forest full grown.

Waking to tree sense,
breeze through my leaves,
xylem flowing
transpiration free.

I hear the birds singing,
a tune to the day.
Their songs my book of hours,
months, years, nights, days.

Sound waves at sea

on the sonic sound-all.
I sway to their themes,
in the wind of my fall,
silent and knowing
there is no need for more.

Until I come to, share this,
trail golden leaves
for a few breaths spoken,
before they're scattered,
guttered, senseless, blown.

* * *

For what am I hoping
with these, my tokens . . .

Haiku

i fished for a word
to set my world in order
stopped still, heard water.

Clearing

I've heard the invisible river of trees. Watched a sea of leaves, waves crash to fields..

I'll miss these garden trees. Their abiding. Their ease with birds, perch for song. I've watched them long, quite rooted, even when wooden to my woodenness with meds. They spoke still, more in silence, deep core to wordgone core. They stayed.

No, some did not, willow's weeping done, now stump, some apple too, gone. Rhododendron scarred. A blight in the air, poison breathed, transmuted into knots by this branch of earth's lung. Gnarled heartwood stases, burl growth. Fire risk.

Now I must unroot, wander, Entish, replant in new ground, hoping to be amongst birds and trees, even bees. To watch and know them, share in my gaze this long dream of gardens, apple, pine, willow, rose tree. Bird shelters, standing their song.

ride

coasted rolls turned rollercoasted
all those moles hammer broken
every day's hall distortion
carni-valed incarnation
waltzered crowds press you on
every ride undodgemable
try them all find your fit
unique you think - become a myth
coasted rolls turn roller coasted
life's freak show tracks
force these tricks
take your place, bearded lady,
clown
got the horror?
ghost train to another town

Grace

"the experience of being delivered from experience"

Martin Luther

a figure awaiting her own sculptress
to deliver her from stone retreat
knows a dream - sun marbled skin uncovered
ease of limbs free to be observed
simply present, still, in every moment
truth ringing through her pose

beginning

sometimes
I feel
my lines
uncover
my humanity

that I
stop
where sanity
begins

nothing
special

just
remedial

now that's
clear

let me
begin

NOTES

* "*Lilly* 4112" - written on a pill.

ACKNOWLEDGEMENTS

A number of poems have appeared elsewhere.

Many have appeared in Survivors' Poetry's Poetry Express Newsletter and at their website (sadly offline at this time). My thanks especially to Dr Simon Jenner for his mentorship and friendship and to all at Survivors' for their unflagging support, including Dave Russell, editor of the Poetry Express Newsletter.

Disability Arts Online (DAO) published an initial selection from my projected full collection and continue to publish my work. My thanks to DAO and especially Colin Hambrook for his and their support and encouragement in publishing essays and poems. https://disabilityarts.online.

The poems 'A Sonnet' and a version of 'Transreality' were published in 2016 in the anthology *Venn* on sexuality and gender from Unstapled Press.

'They Think' was published in 2020 in the anthology *We Are the Change-Makers: poems supporting Drop the Disorder!* edited by Jo Watson from PCCS Books Ltd.

A version of 'Plight' was published in Lapidus International's Spring 2019 Journal.

'A Reunion' was published by The Writers' Cafe Magazine https://thewriterscafemagazine.wordpress.com/ (Issue 17, Masks).

A version of 'Clearing' was published in Caduceus Magazine (Issue 103).

'A Sea' was published by Olney Magazine who featured me as a Poet of the Week in December 2022, https://

www.olneymagazine.com/.

'Tynemouth, Any Mouth' was first published on the Places of Poetry website, https://placesofpoetry.org.uk.

Many of my trans poems have been published by The Beaumont Magazine under my membership name.

I publish poems and other writing at Substack, https://tonihurford.substack.com/ where you're welcome to join the community of my readers.

My thanks to Natalie Scott for her good eye and help in preparing the text, any issues with the final published version are down to me.

I'm grateful to a number of writing groups and adult education classes which humble me and have set me on so many good tracks.

Very special thanks to my friends, family, and all my true helpers.

Printed in Dunstable, United Kingdom

65657997R00031